"There's a reason the 'in case of emergency' instructions on airplanes are illustrations, not simply words—in crisis, the brain grasps images more readily than text. Parker Palmer's wisdom and practical philosophy have guided countless readers through challenges toward a more meaningful life. Sherrill Knezel gives additional depth and visual access to the power of Palmer's inspiring teachings. The paired wisdom of Parker Palmer and the clear, clean, whimsical instructions that Knezel provides for readers, even in the case of an emergency, offer a way to learn twice—by reading and seeing."

Mary Anne Em Radmacher, author of *Courage Doesn't Always Roar*

"*Heart Speak* is a beautiful participatory journey into the depth of self and the soul of society. Palmer's words combined with Knezel's illustrations carefully explore unconscious behaviors, patterns, relationships, and thoughts of everyday existence. This book provides a real road map for clinicians, help groups, parents, families, and friends to contemplate and engage in conversations that lead to movement, growth, and healing. But experience this book for yourself first. It's a true gift!"

Pardeep Singh Kaleka, author and trauma clinician

"Let this book be a gentle light in your day. Savor not only Palmer's magical words and Knezel's beautiful art, but use Knezel's useful prompts to immediately apply the thoughts to your own life."

Julie Causton, CEO of Inclusive Schooling

"Sherrill Knezel is an artist in every sense of the word: Her illustrations winsomely, effectively draw readers into the text. Her personal meditations are wise, vulnerable, and artfully expressed. Her incisive questions beg for deep reflection, contemplation, and response. *Heart Speak* is borne out of the fertile soil of Sherrill's spiritual life and her profound understanding of Parker J. Palmer's classic work *Let Your Life Speak*. She has spoken deeply to my own heart, and I believe she will do the same for you."

Jeff Crosby, author of *The Language of the Soul*

"Sherrill Knezel's new book is visual and verbal encouragement delivered straight to the heart. This collection of thoughts is necessary for our souls at just the right time."

Mike Rohde, author of *The Sketchnote Handbook*

"*Heart Speak* is a stunning journey and invitation, full of compelling words, illustrations, and prompts by both Parker J. Palmer and Sherrill Knezel. *Heart Speak* is full of beauty and truth, and it will no doubt reassure and encourage readers to trust the wisdom that rests within their own hearts. This book is a steady presence on my nightstand, one whose pages I return to over and over again when I need a reminder or reassurance that, most likely, I am on the right path. I can open up to any page and find exactly what I need in the words and images I discover."

Monisha Vasa, psychiatrist and author of *Salve: Words for the Journey*

"I am charmed, delighted, and deeply touched by Sherrill Knezel's *Heart Speak*. The illustrations offer a new and creative dimension to quotes I've treasured for many years. Sherrill's commentary and reflective questions are wonderfully human, tender, thought provoking, and wise. I recommend this book to those who love the work of Parker J. Palmer, but also to anyone who is on the important and curious journey of becoming more fully themself."

Carrie Newcomer, songwriter and author of *The Beautiful Not Yet*

"Sherrill Knezel can transform complicated and complex ideas into deceptively simple–appearing diagrams. But do not be fooled; neither the ideas nor the drawings are simple. This new volume combines her artistic and discerning ability with powerful quotes from Parker J. Palmer. This remarkable blend of talents will reach the heart of verbal and nonverbal learners alike, making these quotes and inspirations accessible to all, so that everyone has an opportunity to understand Palmer's important concepts and apply them. I highly recommend *Heart Speak* as an important tool for self-exploration, self-awareness, and self-care."

Martina Green McGowan, MD, author of *i am the rage*

"When we founded Fall Creek Abbey in 2012, we expectantly placed a copy of *Let Your Life Speak* in each guest room. Without fail, those on retreat would flip through a few pages and be drawn into this small volume, which gently led them into the depths of their own souls. Now we are excited to add this companion resource, *Heart Speak*, as a wise and whimsical guide into the rich invitations found in Palmer's original book. As spiritual directors, we know the value of well-designed, curious questions as well as the gift of visual imagery. Sherrill Knezel's book is a creative doorway into deeper nourishment in fresh, original ways."

David and Beth Booram, directors of Fall Creek Abbey and authors of *When Faith Becomes Sight*

HEART SPEAK

A Visual Interpretation of *Let Your Life Speak*

Sherrill Knezel

in collaboration with

Parker J. Palmer

An imprint of InterVarsity Press
Downers Grove, Illinois

InterVarsity Press
P.O. Box 1400 | Downers Grove, IL 60515-1426
ivpress.com | email@ivpress.com

InterVarsity Press® is the publishing division of InterVarsity Christian Fellowship/USA®. For more information, visit intervarsity.org.

While any stories in this book are true, some names and identifying information may have been changed to protect the privacy of individuals.

Quotations from *Let Your Life Speak* by Parker J. Palmer are used by permission of Jossey-Bass.

Illustrations by the author.

The publisher cannot verify the accuracy or functionality of website URLs used in this book beyond the date of publication.

Cover design and image composite: David Fassett
Interior design: Jeanna Wiggins

ISBN 978-1-5140-0587-3 (print) | ISBN 978-1-5140-0588-0 (digital)

Printed in the United States of America ∞

Library of Congress Cataloging-in-Publication Data
A catalog record for this book is available from the Library of Congress.

9 8 7 6 5 4 3 2 1 | 29 28 27 26 25 24 23 22

For all those seeking:

may you carry with you curiosity,

openness, love, and courage for the journey—

and when your heart speaks ever so softly,

listen well and take good notes.

CONTENTS

PREFACE

Parker J. Palmer

OVER THE PAST FORTY YEARS, I've had the joy of seeing all ten of my books translated into languages I don't read or speak. Whenever a publisher tells me a new translation is in the works, I respond with the same lame joke, whose sole virtue is that it's on me: "That's wonderful! But I still hope we can find someone to translate the book into English."

Now that I've had the good fortune of working with Sherrill Knezel—who's a gifted artist *and* a public school teacher, which makes her one of my culture heroes—I realize that I should have been asking for a visual translation all along! But this one was worth waiting for. I'm very excited about the way Sherrill has used her gifts of art and insight to interpret and express some of the key ideas in *Let Your Life Speak*.

— — ○ — — ○ — — ○ — — ○ — — ○ — — ○ — —

Clearly, images speak to a wider range of people than words alone and are helpful even to "word people" like me. Think of traffic signs that feature an upturned palm that clearly says, "Stop!" or a snake-like line that says, "Caution, sharp turns ahead!" Images incarnate words, making them not only more accessible but more actionable as well. Images instantly deliver a message: "Here's something you need to know to negotiate the road you're on."

The road traveled by *Let Your Life Speak* is now relatively long, as such things go. Now in its early twenties, the book has spoken to readers from several generations. I smiled when I learned that Sherrill found the book in her husband's grandmother's library. I receive a quiet flow of notes from middleaged people telling me how glad they are that a parent or grandparent urged them to read the book. I also hear from recent high school or college grads, saying that the book came to them as a course assignment or as a graduation present.

It's a special delight to hear "full circle" stories like one I read a month or two ago: "In 2002, I gave this book to my grandson when he got out of college. Now he's 40, and has an 18-year-old son, my great grandson. My son gave the book to his son for high school graduation, and now we're talking about it together." Stories like that warm my heart, even though they make me feel very old!

With the publication of Sherrill Knezel's graphic translation, which may well speak to an even younger set, I aim to live long enough to get a note like this from someone who turned twelve in 2022: "My sixth-grade teacher used this book in class, and I'm still thinking about some of the things we talked about back then."

My gratitude goes to the hundreds of thousands of readers who have used the book to help them hear their own lives speak. They have encouraged me to keep listening to my life, a practice that never fails me if I have the patience to listen long enough.

My gratitude also goes to Sherrill Knezel who had the idea for this translation. It's been a joy to work with her and to have my eyes opened to the many ways images can help us speak and listen. I have every reason to believe that you, the reader, will have the same experience.

An Invitation

THIS BOOK IS MEANT to journey alongside Parker J. Palmer's book *Let Your Life Speak*—to uplift and amplify Parker's work in a new way and provide a creative visual access point to the book that has been a steadfast companion to me through the years.

When I was a young parent and new teacher, my husband's grandmother Janet gave me one of Parker's earlier books *The Courage to Teach.* I devoured it. Janet and I had many conversations in her small kitchen over tea discussing the themes and threads in the book. Janet was insatiably curious and always had piles of books for us to talk about when I visited. When she passed, I inherited several of these treasured books—*Let Your Life Speak* being one of them. As I started reading, it took only a few pages, with pencil in hand, to strongly sense that I would read and reread *Let Your Life Speak* many times in the coming years.

I couldn't have known how true that would be. As I started following Parker's work and reading more of his books, I found myself returning to *Let Your Life Speak* whenever I was feeling unmoored and in need of grounding or needed to be reminded of the importance of stillness and inner work. I kept it close at hand as I started a daily drawing and meditation practice of illustrating an inspiring or spiritual quote in the predawn hours while savoring that first cup of cinnamon coffee.

Parker's words found their way into my first collection of morning drawings. So when I learned of the Growing Edge Retreats he co-led with Carrie Newcomer, I knew I would apply as a fiftieth birthday present to myself—and hope like heck I would get accepted! And I did!

Since drawing is how I listen, process, and make meaning, I sketch-noted the entire transformative and soul-filled weekend in March 2019. Somewhere among the powerful circle conversations, poetry readings, and collaborative song-writing, an idea took root: *Parker and I are going to write a book together.*

After returning home from the weekend retreat, the idea kept tugging at my heart, so I reached out to Parker to pitch my idea—I asked permission to create a visual interpretation of seventy-plus passages from *Let Your Life Speak*—the only effort on his part would be to say yes. To my delight, he did, and to my even bigger delight, we began meeting virtually as I worked on the images and got further into the process of publishing. Getting to know Parker—his generosity, wisdom, and humor—has been a true gift of writing this book.

I find immense joy in gathering inspiring words and laying them down interpreted as simple and graceful lines, shapes, and spaces that help me make sense of the world. I also am completely in love with beautiful questions that open worlds within and help us speak our best selves into being. I like to think of this book as a conversation with Parker and myself spoken through images, personal reflections, and questions that invite you to sit with them, reflect, and hopefully visit again and again. The words placed within the images on the left-hand pages are Parker's. The words on the right-hand pages are my musings and questions in response.

I invite you to take this book in your pocket and read it in the way that nurtures you. Open to a random page. Or read it cover to cover. Write and draw in the margins. Bend and bookmark the pages. Talk with God (or Creator, Universe, or whatever name you use to refer to a higher power) about what you are noticing. Share it with a friend. Discuss it with a small group. Pull it out when you need a reminder of our true and precious work in this world—which I believe is to be in relationship with each other—in all its messy and beautiful and sacred forms.

It is my deepest hope that the drawings will expand your connection with Parker's words and that the book will be a gentle light in your day, a salve for your soul, reminding you that you are not alone, and that community *is* abundance. Perhaps it will encourage and empower you to listen to what your heart has been speaking all along.

1

LISTENING
TO LIFE

Before you tell your
life what you intend
to do with it, listen
for what it intends
to do with you.

I have gotten myself into trouble trying to be everything for everybody, and in the end, helping no one. I assigned self-worth only when I was doing or helping or being what someone else or society told me I should be. When I listen quietly though, and allow for what wants to emerge, that is when I can gently hold life's hand. Charging in with expectations often blinds me to the gentle possibilities that are in a tender beginning stage. Open . . . breathe . . . stay for a moment and receive.

What wants to emerge for you? How might you make time to nurture that new and tender growth?

True self, when violated,
will always resist us,
Sometimes at great cost,
holding our lives in check
until we honor its truth.

I have learned that when I deny my true self, all sorts of interesting things happen . . . and that is putting it mildly! When I push on and do what I think others expect of me instead of listening to that quiet voice inside, I put my mind, body, and soul at peril. I learned this lesson loud and clear when I denied the stress I was under a few years ago, and my body decided for me that I needed to lay down due to back pain. I was resisting speaking up about my own needs and desires and putting my health at risk in the process. This continues to be a growing edge for me, but I listen quicker these days when my body and soul speak.

Think of a moment when you knowingly denied your true voice or true self. Where did you feel that physically? What teachings arose from that experience?

Running beneath the surface of the experience I call my life, there is a deeper & truer life waiting to be acknowledged.

Making time and space to truly listen for the life that wants to emerge is not selfish or wasteful. It is how I begin to acknowledge the more meaningful and true life that I may not even have words to describe just yet. Being open to surprise and wonder . . . even expecting them to show up, is a way to adventure into a new day. When I wonder what delightful connection or simple, ordinary beauty I will experience today, I find that I am more intentional about seeking joy in small moments.

When have you been surprised by a beautiful moment? Recall the moment and what it meant to you.

The words we speak
often contain counsel
we are trying to give
ourselves.

Oh, how I have decided so many times that I have the answer for other people's problems . . . that I have the wisdom to fix what they don't even feel is broken. When I recognize that I need to start with my own inner work (since that is the only thing I am in control of!), I find that I breathe easier and can make better use of my energy. I don't have enough fingers and toes to count the number of times I have said to a friend, "Be gentle with yourself," only to turn around and do the opposite when I am struggling with fear or failure. I have realized that my way of processing life is by connecting with others who create a safe space for me to give words to my thoughts. The true practice is to listen to my own counsel, to go within instead of without and trust my own guidance.

What might you say to yourself the next time you are struggling with fear or feeling overwhelmed? (Hint: pretend you are talking to your closest and dearest friend.) What would be helpful and what would not be helpful?

The soul speaks its
truth only under quiet,
inviting, & trustworthy
conditions.

Allowing is a hard thing for me. Can I make the time to be quiet and invite my soul to feel comfortable enough to speak? To feel safe enough to be seen and heard and to trust myself enough to emerge? When I truly embrace the fact that I am the source of time, I relax into the space where inner work can begin. I always say that my blissful place is in, on, or near water. It is where I do my best thinking and best self-care, for that matter. It is where I can sink into my body and listen to my soul. When I am feeling anxious, I know I have not made time to walk to the nearby river, sit on my favorite rock by its edge, and invite my soul to speak.

What are the best conditions for you to create a safe and brave space to listen to your own soul speak?

2

NOW I BECOME MYSELF

What a long time it
can take to become
the person one has
always been.

At each age and stage, I felt I had arrived. When I graduated, got married, had children, started my own business . . . you name it, I marked the event as a placeholder—proof that I was the full me. Once I accepted (embraced) that the beautiful thing about becoming yourself is that it is both an infinitely forgiving and ongoing process, then I could unlearn all the stories I had chosen to tell myself and remember who I had always been.

What story do you need to unlearn to remember your true self?

Today I understand
vocation quite differently
—not as a goal to be
achieved but as a gift
to be received.

Vocation, for me, has emerged concurrently with my own becoming. As I have made space for radical listening to my inner voice, only the things that I couldn't *not* do were left as I sifted out all of the other things I felt I should do. Listening, creating, teaching, and connecting are all parts of my vocation. It is a gift to find vocation and a practice to receive it. The true and difficult work for me has always been the receiving part.

What has been your understanding of vocation? What can you do to create space to invite it to emerge?

The deepest vocational question is not "what ought I to do with my life?" It is the more elemental and demanding "Who am I?" "What is my nature?"

These questions require me to do what I call some "serious sitting" with and in my own stuff. I need to peel away the "shoulds" that have accumulated because I have carried the stories others have told for me about who I am. The middle-child-people-pleaser in me has a hard time with this. I discover more questions that arise for me. Who do I want to be in the world and how do I want to move through today? How can I embrace my own true self to help uplift and amplify others in this world?

What questions surface for you?

Our deepest calling is
to grow into our own
authentic self-hood, whether
or not it conforms to
some image of who we
ought to be.

I have a vision of myself buried under the weight of expectations (of others and self-imposed), of all the "shoulds" and what-would-others-think boulders I carry. The work is to remove the weight that no longer serves me—to refuse to deny the small voice within that says, "Yes . . . yes . . . this is me and it feels like home." For me, these places look like listening, drawing, and uplifting others doing transformational work in community.

What parts of you feel like home? What might it look or feel like to set down the "ought to be" parts?

Challendes..., largely beyond our control, can strip the ego of the illusion that it is in control & make space for true self to emerge.

I remember reading a quote that went something like this: "If you want to make God (or the universe) laugh, make plans." I've learned to hold my plans and expectations very gently, knowing full well that life is impermanent, uncertain, and chaotic at times. The less tightly I hold on to my expectations and plans, the less pain I experience when they inevitably change. Here again, allowing serves me well. Even embracing the change and laughing at my ego for having thought I was in control!

What challenge in your life has brought valuable teaching for you?

But as pilgrims must
discover if they are to
complete their quest,
we are led to our truth
by our weaknesses as
well as our strengths.

I realize that my weakness is not being present. Wanting to be somewhere, do something, help someone. Understanding comes when I dig further and grasp that what I am really doing is avoiding sitting with what *is*. I am enough even when I am still . . . especially when I am still. The practice of being still with myself has led to the ability to be still in the presence of another. Deep listening is a strength I consider sacred.

What do you consider a weakness? What strength has it accompanied in your life?

Vocation at its deepest level is, "This is something I can't not do..."

What are the things you can't not do? For me, it is teaching, drawing, listening deeply, making connections between ideas, people, and heart songs. It is allowing and receiving, loving, and appreciating. It is feeling the joy, beauty, sorrow, and all the things in between in this one amazing life.

What is something that you can't not do?

The moment was large
with things I needed
to learn.

Whew. It has been a practice of mine to sit with an emotion or a moment. The difficult ones, I would rather walk away from and avoid altogether, but they pass. That is the one true thing about all of them: the joy and the sorrow are impermanent. When I appreciate that simple fact, it makes life sweeter. It opens a moment for all it can teach me.

Can you name a moment that was large with learnings for you? Perhaps the learnings were immediate and perhaps they have been years in arriving.

Self-care is never a selfish act—it is simply good stewardship of the only gift I have, the gift I was put on earth to offer others.

I was forced to completely reframe my views on self-care when I experienced back issues several years ago. It was in the midst of lots of stress and change in my life and I was caring for everyone and every situation but myself. I carried lots of things that weren't mine to carry. Thinking I could fix everything, I ignored small warning signs from my body until I received a loud and clear message that came at the end of a yoga class, of all places. I had done a forward fold and felt a twinge. The next morning, I was in so much pain that I had to lay down in my kitchen while trying to make breakfast. I tried for a while to keep going . . . teaching, parenting, organizing, but at long last I realized I needed to just lay down and rest. It felt like God had pointed a finger at my chest and said, "Stop!" In the weeks ahead I would learn how to release, surrender, and receive. I would learn how to accept help and I would learn that it is not weakness, but pure strength and confidence in self to do so. Self-care became the only way to heal physically and emotionally. Now when I feel my body speaking, I am quick to listen. If I don't, I have no gifts to give.

What does self-care look like for you? What are the signs that tell you it is time to practice it?

I will no longer act on
the outside in a way
that contradicts the
truth I hold deeply on
the inside.

We have all met people whose inner and outer selves do not match. They spend lots of time and energy trying to determine what others want of them and try to become that person. For me, it became too much work to live a divided life—worrying what others thought, being overwhelmed by the "shoulds" (my own and others). I wanted to listen to and speak from my heart in all situations. This has become my work. To strive to be myself through and through. It is a lifelong process, but it is among the worthiest of pursuits for me.

When do you feel your inner truth matches your outer words and actions? Who are you with? What are you doing?

I will no longer act
as if I were less
than the whole person
I know myself inwardly
to be.

This is an ongoing process . . . two steps forward, one step back at any given moment. Just when I think I am making good progress and growth in this practice, I realize I am falling back into my default of making sure everyone is okay in the moment and reading the room for what others need instead of creating loving boundaries that allow my inner self to match my outer self.

What is one true aspect of yourself you know inwardly that you aspire to share outwardly with others?

No reward anyone might
give us could possibly
be greater than the
reward that comes
from living by our own
best lights.

There is a deep satisfaction in being comfortable in my own skin. The journey of becoming more myself is in itself a reward. Being able to look back on where I've been, who I was, and how far I've come is the true evidence of growth. It's then that I often say to myself, "Well done, me!"

What is one thing you've done recently that deserves a "Yay, YOU!"?

But every journey, honestly undertaken, stands a chance of taking us toward the place where our deep gladness meets the world's deep need.

What brings me deep gladness is creating, teaching, deep listening, collaboration, and drawing out conversations to increase connection and clarity between humans. When I stumbled on the field of graphic recording so many of these things came together for me, and I realized it was something I needed to pursue. Using images and text to uplift and amplify generative and transformational work being done to build community brings me joy.

Where is this intersection for you? If you haven't found it yet, how might you get curious about exploring where to look for it?

3

WHEN
WAY
CLOSES

"...way has never opened in front of me.... But a lot of way has closed behind me & that's had the same guiding effect."

I remember learning this lesson when I started my business. I was trying to force the places and people I worked with, almost begging them to see my worth. Many doors closed . . . some quietly and some with a SLAM. Looking back now, the doors that closed were a blessing and their closing led to other more meaningful openings.

Can you name a recent door closing that has had a guiding effect for you? What learning was brought about by the closing door?

Sometimes the "shoulds"
do not work because
the life one is living
runs crosswise to
one's soul.

I carried "shoulds" for a long time and still catch myself picking up some that aren't mine to carry. I have learned to check in with my body and try on a decision like a new coat. Does it feel right? If I were to do this thing, where and how would it register physically for me? Sometimes I know immediately. Other times I feel like I have walked through a cobweb and need to brush it off, extricating myself from a yes that should have been a no. I find the phrase, "Not a match," coming out of my mouth. That is when I know that the decision is running crosswise to my soul.

What physical feeling do you get when you listen to "shoulds" instead of your soul? What is one step you can take to move less crosswise?

We can learn as much
about our nature by
running into our limits
as by experiencing our
potentials.

I had a high school design class teacher who would assign projects with what I felt were ridiculous constraints. For one assignment, the prompt was to create a series of small abstract compositions using three shapes, two colors, and one pattern in each design. I have forgotten the other specifics of the assignment, but I remember the feeling of frustration. When I said something about it, the teacher replied, "Sometimes you have to be creative to be creative." Whew. I have since come to love the challenge of bumping up against my limits. These obstacles force me to get clear on my values, to sit with my ego in some discomfort, and then get on with being creative to be creative.

How have you run into your own limits and navigated the obstacles they presented?

There are some roles & relationships in which we thrive & others in which we wither & die.

I used to scoff at the "reason, season, lifetime" saying that references different types of friendships in our lives until I personally experienced a "season" friendship. I struggled with the story I told myself around it—how it was a commentary on my ability to be a good friend—but came to the realization that it wasn't a good fit anymore. I wasn't thriving in the relationship, and neither was the other person. Recognizing that the conditions in our relationships may not be working is the first step to making positive change.

What kind of conditions in a relationship help you thrive?

Give only if you have
something you must
give; give only if you
are someone for whom
giving is its own reward.

I take great pleasure in finding something simple and beautiful to give to someone—a small bouquet of flowers from my yard, a decadent bar of chocolate, a handmade piece of art I've created, a handwritten note. I run into trouble when I say yes but really mean no, or when I allow the "shoulds" to overrun my gut instinct. Giving from a place of guilt only leaves a trail of resentment instead of giving from a place of love.

What is a memory you have of giving when the act itself was the reward? What was the gift you gave?

Burnout, in my experience
results from trying to
give what I do not
possess.

I have come to value generosity as a character trait, but there are times when the most generous thing I can do for myself is to *not* give. To allow an opportunity to help someone pass me by and instead make time to rest or reflect. This runs counter to some serious German Catholic conditioning from my childhood. The unspoken mantra was, "You are what you accomplish in a day." But my personal experience was that I became resentful and depleted when I gave time and energy from a place of emptiness. It has taken me years to learn that I am worthy of love and belonging even when I am resting ... especially then, for that is the only way I can replenish my reserves so I can truly give.

What has your experience been around burnout? What learnings have you brought forward from it?

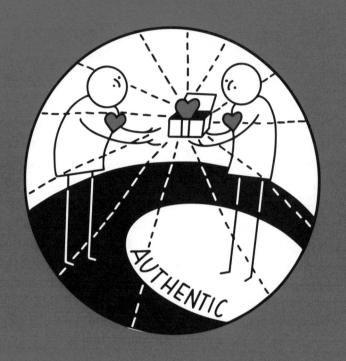

When the gift I have
to give to the other is
integral to my own nature,
...it will renew itself,
—and me—even as I
give it away.

When a fellow church member assumed I was adept at calligraphy and asked me to write out certificates for memorial gifts made to the church, instead of saying no, I taught myself rudimentary calligraphy and did them. But all the while I was muttering to myself because my heart wasn't in it. In contrast, when a family member was looking for an original piece of art to gift to a friend who was celebrating a new beginning, I loved creating a commissioned piece using a favorite quote. Listening, drawing, cooking . . . these are gifts I have to give and enjoy giving. It is when I say yes to things that are not aligned with what I consider my gifts that I begin feeling resentful or angry. It is then that I find the negative self-talk creeps in.

What is one of your gifts that you love to share with others? What is one moment that you felt rejuvenated giving it?

We will become better
teachers not by trying
to fill the potholes in
our souls, but by knowing
them so well that we
can avoid them.

Giving to others without feeling fulfilled or rested myself is a huge pothole for me when the only purpose of giving is the feeling that I "should" give. When I feel resentful for saying yes to helping, the "Danger! Potholes Ahead" road sign glaringly appears in my mind's eye. In that moment when I recognize why I'm angry, that's the true moment of learning. *Oh yeah, I remember this*, I think. That's also when I can step back and gently decline an opportunity to help and gain a better understanding of myself and others.

What is one pothole in your soul that you seem to hit every time? How can you embrace and avoid it?

If we are to live our
lives fully & well, we
must learn to embrace
the opposites, to live in
creative tension between
our limits & our potentials.

I learned from mentors I've had over the years that constraints can be the exact creative impetus we need to think outside the box. As I began to teach art in my own classroom years later, I came to realize this firsthand. Whenever I taught a clay or painting unit with elementary students and gave no directions except "make whatever you want," the results were usually awful. Clear expectations are useful and kind for all artists (and humans, for that matter). Constraints can become the guardrails that keep us on track and challenge us to reach our potential in spite of or *because* of them.

Can you name something in your life that has felt like a limit but led to you holding the creative tension long enough to achieve something you didn't think possible?

4

ALL
THE WAY
DOWN

One begins the slow
walk back to health
by choosing each day
things that enliven one's
selfhood & resisting
things that do not.

When I choose to act or speak in a way that doesn't align with my values or soul, I feel it in my stomach. It starts as a twinge and I try to tell myself it is nothing, but my body knows the truth. "Shoulds" weigh heavily on me and getting curious about how I carry my own and others' "shoulds" has been a way to discover simple things that bring joy—the first warm cup of coffee before the world wipes sleep from its eyes, a well-worn beloved book penciled and drawn in the margins, a vulnerable conversation with a dear friend, a kindergartener's unabashed use of color in their art and the pure enthusiasm of it.

What is a small thing that enlivens you? How can you resist or release one thing that doesn't?

Depression is the
ultimate state of
disconnection, not
only between people, &
between mind & heart,
but between one's self-
image & public mask.

Disconnection is what can send me into anguish. Surface relationships tire me out. But what my real inner work has focused on is making inner match outer. For me an honest and vulnerable conversation with a friend is one of the most sacred acts—to hold space and deeply listen to another human vulnerably and courageously reveal their heart—scars and all. To do this, I have found I must make sure my own mind and heart are one and that I have released the need to curate who and how I am in the world.

Who are you when you are your truest, best self? Do you share that with the world or edit it to make it easier for others? How might it feel to release the need to curate who and how you are in the world?

One of the hardest things
we must do sometimes is
to be present to another
person's pain without trying
to "fix" it, to simply stand
respectfully at the edge of
that person's mystery
and misery.

Every fiber of my being seems to want to fix other peoples' hurts. I feel deeply, whether it is my own emotions or those of others in the room, and at times it can be exhausting. As a self-diagnosed empath, it is an ongoing practice for me to create and hold space for people in my life without feeling like I need to do something to help. It can be such a gift to both the giver and receiver to simply and respectfully companion another in their joy or pain.

When have you felt truly companioned during a difficult time? What did it look, sound, and feel like? How can you give that same gift to another?

The poet Rainer Maria Rilke says, "love...consists in this, that two solitudes protect & border & salute each other."

Relationships of any kind can test the truth and necessity of solitude. Rilke's use of "solitudes" seems to make synonymous the aloneness of being with ourselves and of human beings in general. I came to the realization that time away from a friend, a spouse, or a family member often allowed each of us to refresh, refuel, and grow in ways that may not or could not happen when we were together. It was not for lack of love that I began to embrace this protecting, bordering, and saluting a loved one's solitude, but instead, it grew out of immense respect and love for that person.

What comes up for you when you first think of solitude? When has someone afforded you the space and solitude you needed and how did you feel? How can you gift this to another?

Do you think you could see it instead as the hand of a friend, pressing you down to the ground on which it is safe to stand?

Getting to stable ground is a comforting way to look at a humbling event. It is easy to see the glass half empty when facing a situation that didn't go as I expected. When my reality ends up far from the expectations I held, I experience pain. How long the pain lasts and the intensity of it is directly proportional to the time it takes me to reframe the situation and change the narrative. This has been transformational for me time and time again.

What situation have you faced (or are you facing) that you can reframe? Can you be open to seeing it in a new light? What if you gently set down the old story in preparation for a new one to emerge?

The grace of being
pressed down to the
ground is also simple:
when we slip & fall, it is
usually not fatal, & we
can get back up.

Taking small risks, trying new things, being open and willing to fail in order to learn and grow . . . all of these have gifted me grace. Am I consistent about moving in the world this way? Not always. Doing things that are uncomfortable and certainly on my growing edge takes courage and fortitude. It is easier to stay in a safe space—do things the way I have always done them—but this is never where I find the magic of surprise and serendipity. Saying yes to something I don't quite know how to do is a sure way to learn some things about myself.

Can you think of a moment when you stepped out of your comfort zone? What did it feel like? What did you learn about yourself?

True self is true friend.
One ignores or rejects
such friendship only
at one's peril.

Finding my true self has been an ongoing endeavor and can be elusive when I am listening too intently to others—scanning the landscape for how I think I ought to be. I pick up the roles others project on me and ignore my true self calling, the self that waits for me to stop . . . rest . . . listen. During a time in my life, I disregarded that call to listen, and my body decided to force me to literally stop everything for weeks and just lie down. I learned intimately that mind, body, and soul (true self) are connected and that there is true peril in NOT befriending myself.

What has been your experience when you have disregarded your true self? How can you be a friend to yourself in some small way today?

Self is... a common mix of good & evil, darkness & light, a place where we can finally embrace the humanity we share with others.

I grew up with the belief that people are either good or bad. You had to be selfless and giving to be considered good and anything different was selfish. I internalized that as I grew into adulthood and it led to the belief that I was only worthy of love if I was helping, giving to, or fixing others. What a heavy way to move about in this world. As I embraced curiosity and questioned why I was this way, I slowly learned of the concept of duality and that I needed to allow in *all* the parts of myself. Only when I could accept the dark and the light of my own being was I able to see the shared humanity that connects us.

What parts of yourself have you exiled that you could gently allow in? What might it feel or look like to embrace shared humanity with a friend, neighbor, or stranger?

When you truly possess
all you have been &
done...you are fierce
with reality.

I used to take pride in being the teacher, parent, friend who had it all together and could keep every plate spinning. I would anticipate what my children, friends, or family needed and offer help before they asked. Then the plates started falling when life got to be too much. I tried to keep going, not being willing to set down the identity I had hidden behind. Who was I if I wasn't helping others? And who was I to need or accept help? When I was forced to sit with these questions, I realized that I was the being—not the doing. I was forced to accept all that I had been and done, and I was stronger, gentler, and more compassionate for it.

Can you name a moment when you denied mistakes instead of embracing them? How might you allow and embrace who you are in one small way today?

When I started attending to my own truth, more of that truth became available in my work & relationships.

I had been a filler of silences until I realized doing so was a way to avoid my own truth. On a recent walk to a favorite spot by a river near my house, I enjoyed the quiet of a gray early morning, soft with the spaciousness and possibility of a new day. Learning to get still, allow, and then truly listen to my own heart and spirit gifts me more energy to be present as I move through my day.

What whisper of your own truth have you heard lately? How can you attend to your own truth in a small and gentle way today?

Whatever's been uprooted,
let it be seedbed for
the growing that's to
come. I plowed to unearth
last year's reasons—
The farmer plows to plant
a greening season.

I have felt unmoored these past few years as fear and uncertainty have been unwanted companions. When I feel myself closing to protect my heart from vulnerability and difficult emotions, I remind myself gently, "Open, open, open." This simple phrase (along with some good breathing) has saved me time and again and led to connections I couldn't have predicted. Perhaps the turning over of an experience and the releasing of an expectation that no longer serves me are just what I need to begin again.

Can you recall a moment when you felt unmoored? How might you reframe it so that you can see it as a necessary preparation for a "greening season"?

5

LEADING
FROM
WITHIN

If it is true that we are
made for community,
then leadership is
everyone's vocation.

I have always referred to myself as a reluctant leader. I prefer to do what needs to be done in the background without acknowledgment and I struggle to graciously receive a compliment. I have come to realize this is a false narrative about myself. It is human nature to want to be seen and heard, and we each bring unique gifts and talents to the world. Leaning into those gifts and sharing them with the community that surrounds us is what vocation and leadership are all about.

Have you had the experience of being a reluctant leader? What were the circumstances? How can you embrace a role of leadership in one of the communities you are a part of?

I lead by word & deed
simply because I am here
doing what I do.

Leader is such a big word. Perhaps this is why I have shied away from situations where someone uses it to refer to me. Maybe it's the fear of not being able to handle the expectations that accompany the role or the worry that I won't do or be enough. Reframing leadership as "doing what I do" makes the role right-sized for me. Be myself? Uplift others? Pitch in and do what needs to be done? That I can do, and if that is what leadership is, then I'm all in and we truly *are* all leaders.

What words or deeds have you recently shared or received that were meaningful for you? What are you already doing or being that is leading by word or deed?

A leader is someone with the power to project either shadow or light onto some part of the world & onto the lives of the people who dwell there.

I am a self-diagnosed empath and profoundly affected by people in general. Our words, actions, and energy have such power to tear down or build up. A leader I work with once casually said to me, "You are meant for greatness!" I wanted to look over my shoulder to see who she was talking about. I left the conversation with a changed view of myself, touched that someone saw such potential in me even when I did not. I'm sure she had no idea the power of her words, but those very words have given me courage over the years to take risks, speak up, and put myself and my ideas out into the world. To think that I have that same power to make someone's day is a gift and awesome responsibility I do not take lightly.

Can you remember a time when someone's words left a positive impact on you? How might you use the power of your words and actions to project light onto some part of the world today? What one way can you uplift a friend or stranger whose path you cross today?

If we do not understand
that the enemy is within,
we will find a thousand
ways of making someone
"out there" into the enemy.

When I am struggling with my own insecurities, doubts, and fears, I default to blaming others or avoidance. This is my enemy—my own personal darkness. It is the nature of humans to react to pain or discomfort with the fight or flight response and I am certainly not exempt ... in fact, I couldn't be more textbook. This malady has been in the world writ large of late. So many people in pain and fear have created harmful and vitriolic divisions by "othering" those different from themselves instead of doing the necessary inner work. A recent change for me has been that I am able to more quickly notice and name when I turn to blaming and avoiding. "Oh, yes—here I am running away from a hard conversation again, blaming someone else for my own discomfort." I remind myself to stay, to sit with fear, hold its hand even, and remind myself again and again to look within.

What is your default reaction to difficult conversations with those who have a differing opinion or perspective from yours? Do you protect your heart by avoidance or armoring? How might you open in curiosity to both your own reaction and another's lived experience?

If you can't get out
of it, get into it!

Parker Palmer tells the story of his Outward Bound experience rappelling down the face of a cliff and at one point being paralyzed by fear. One of the guides shares the Outward Bound motto, telling him in effect to "get into it" in order to get down to safe ground.

I have vivid memories of early on in my work as a graphic recorder, standing in front of a huge blank piece of paper, my hands filled with markers, my back to a large room of conference attendees ready to hear a compelling keynote, and my heart and mind racing. My job was to listen deeply to capture the big ideas using images and text on the paper, but my mind and heart had other ideas—who was I to be standing here doing this? How would I do the speaker justice? What if I missed something? My practice to survive my paralyzing fear became this: take three deep breaths, touch the blank paper, and repeat my own mantra, "Not to me, but through me." I trusted that whatever words and ideas needed to be on the drawing I was creating would come through me, and I gave myself permission for it to be imperfect. This was my way of getting into it and I have continued this practice each time since.

Can you name a moment when you needed to make the choice to "get into it"? What were you feeling in your body? What advice would you give a dear friend (or yourself!) when faced with a can't-get-out-of-it situation?

On the inward and
downward spiritual journey,
the only way out is in
and through.

I have looked to favorite books and poetry for guidance and wayfinding along my own inward and downward spiritual journey. Sage traveling wisdom from others who have done their own inner work has accompanied me on the path in and through. The journey has required me to sit with discomfort, embrace it with gentle curiosity, and allow myself plenty of detours and missteps along the way. The quickest way for me to learn something is to learn exactly how *not* to do it. My reminders to myself along the way have been simple: breathe, open, allow, surrender. These words have given me agency and fortitude to continue.

What brings you joy or comfort during hard times? What reminders to yourself would be helpful for your own journey in and through?

When we are insecure about our own identities, we create settings that deprive other people of their identities as a way of buttressing our own.

I am an identical twin, a middle child, and an empath—three interesting identities that have tilted my personality scale toward insecurity and a struggle to speak my own truth. I tend to read the energy of the room and figure out what others need first before building up enough courage to stand in my own power. When I find myself judging others harshly, it is always in direct proportion to how unsure or uncomfortable I am feeling in my own skin. Conversely, I am the best version of myself when I feel seen and heard.

I have seen this play out in my own classroom throughout years of teaching elementary art. A student who feels insecure or left out may bully another student to feel powerful. When small children are in pain or fear, behavior is often the only form of communication they may have access to. I have found that moving alongside a student, asking a gentle question, then listening and giving a child choice or agency works wonders. This is true for kindergarteners and adults alike.

How does it feel in your body when you are unsure or uncertain? How might you create the conditions for yourself, a friend, or a loved one to feel uplifted?

The great community asks
us to do only what we
are able & trust the rest
to other hands.

So often I have gotten myself into trouble trying to do or carry something that wasn't mine. I have listened to the "shoulds" or tried to fix someone else because that is what caring, compassionate friends, sisters, partners do. That narrative was an ill-fitting garment I wore for many years. Now when I catch myself creeping back into carrying what isn't mine, I remind myself that often all another human being needs or wants is to be seen, heard, and accompanied—not fixed. Community is strengthened when we trust and empower each other to offer what we can, knowing that who we are is enough.

What gifts do you possess that are right-sized offerings to community? What might it look like to trust that others will do the same?

Chaos is the
precondition
to creativity.

I am a procrastinator at heart, and I know that I need a deadline or things don't get done. Even then, I tend to organize a drawer or clean out a closet before I start the task I *really* should be doing. Perhaps this is my way of trying to keep the chaos of fear and self-doubt that are frequently my precursor to creating at bay, but it is also a way of preparing to create. I soon realize that cleaning a physical space is my way of avoiding the inner work necessary to begin, and can laugh at my straightening. Acknowledging the chaos and allowing the next step to be incremental is as good a start as any.

What readying do you do before embarking on a journey or task? What does the moment feel like when you are able to begin? How can this inform what you need?

A good scientist does not fear the death of a hypothesis because that "failure" clarifies the steps that need to be taken toward truth...

I talk with my elementary art students early and often about the similarities between artists and scientists … they both observe closely, experiment freely, and embrace mistakes to learn and grow. Removing the fear of failure for young students empowers them to use their imagination and create wildly uninhibited art. I wish I could paint with confidence and abandon like a kindergartener! Children's author Barney Saltzburg calls it a "beautiful oops" when you make a mistake in art and then turn it into something else. He encourages young artists to turn them into something they might not have thought of before. Oh, what a fantastic reframe!

Shortly after learning this phrase, one of my kindergarteners dripped paint where she didn't want it. As she fixed it by adding legs to turn it into an insect, she exclaimed, "Look! I'm beautiful oopsing!" When we can release fear of mistakes, it opens a clear path toward creativity and truth … and maybe even a bit of fun along the way.

Can you remember a time when you made a mistake that led to learning and growth? What if you reframed your next mistake or "beautiful oops"? How might that change the feeling of the experience?

By allowing something
to die when its time
is due, we create the
conditions under which
new life can emerge.

"This is how we've always done it!" It's a phrase most of us have heard at work, school, church, or any organization or community where humans congregate and collaborate. Things can be done the same way . . . until they aren't, and even though there is discomfort in and aversion to change, the releasing of old ways creates the space for new ideas to take shape. The world pandemic has taught us as a global community that we can change quickly and learn new ways to connect, communicate, and create.

What is one idea or way of doing something in your life that might have served its purpose and is now time to release? How might this action of letting go seed new growth?

If people skimp on their inner work, their outer work will suffer as well.

I can always tell when I have not prioritized my own inner work. I get short with others, eat poorly, and let go of moving my body regularly. It isn't until I realize that my mind is filled with spiraling negative thoughts and worries that I stop myself long enough to name how I am feeling or what I am doing. "Oh, this is me feeling lonely or unappreciated." Then I can begin again to take care of myself. That often looks like what helps keep a plant healthy—enough water, sunlight, and a few gentle words.

What does it look like when you are skimping on your own inner work? How might you gently course-correct when you realize it is happening?

We must come together
in ways that respect the
solitude of the soul, that
avoid the unconscious
violence we do when we
try to save each other.

While my tendency is to be a helper and fixer, that changed when a dear friend lost her husband. There was nothing I could do or say to make anything better. What I did learn to do was to sit alongside her, protecting and respecting the solitude she needed to navigate deep grief. I learned that sometimes hurting humans can't tell you what would be helpful, but they can often tell you what isn't helpful. Accept that as truth. I learned that presence is enough and listening is an act of love. In the process, I also learned to inhabit and respect my own solitude as well.

How do you find yourself reacting when a friend or loved one is in pain? What does your response tell you about what you think you "should" do to help versus what that person might actually need?

We can remind each other... of all the ways that fear forecloses the potentials.

When I am in fear, I find myself "what-if"-ing a lot. I can spiral, which will raise my heart rate and make my palms sweat just by thinking of worst-case scenarios. I remember hearing an interview with a brain researcher who stated that our body doesn't know the difference when we "what-if." It reacts physically as if the bad thing had happened. Thoughts are powerful things! I am learning to imagine the best-case scenario instead. What if things go wildly well? Reminding my heart to open, open more, and stay open is immensely helpful. Doing that for each other can be generative and transformational.

How does fear manifest itself for you physically? How might it feel to best-case scenario "what-if" instead?

...we do not need to
BE the fear we have.

As a new teacher, a new graphic recorder, a new workshop facilitator, I would find myself in what I called "Who am I" situations. Who was I to be doing what I was about to do? When were the "real" experts going to step in? The fear was real, but I would do the thing anyway. I was sharing this with a business coach a few years ago and she said it sounded like I was in a "Why not me" phase and what I needed to get to was an "Of course me" phase. That made me smile. Now when I am nervous facing a new situation, I think, *Of course me!*

Can you think of one person in your life who could benefit from hearing this story? Psst . . . tell yourself and then pass it on.

6

THERE IS A SEASON

We are here not only
to transform the world
but also to be transformed.

There are those that choose a "word of the year" each January. I have resisted this practice, but last year the word *allow* tugged at me. At first, my ego showed up as I questioned if I should choose a bolder word, such as "create," "inspire," or "lead." However, the more I settled into what it would mean to allow and embrace life, the more I believed my chosen word would require strength, courage, vulnerability, and humility. I'd need to be open and honest about my own strengths and capacities and ask for help when needed. The ebb and flow of seasons are so fitting as a metaphor encouraging me to enjoy each moment, but also to release what I no longer need to allow for growth and change. When I allowed myself to be transformed by joy, grief, or solitude, then and only then could I contribute in a positive, generative way.

Describe a big or small moment when you felt transformed. How did it inspire you to transform part of your world?

What does nature do in
autumn? It scatters the
seeds that will bring new
growth in spring — and
scatters them with
amazing abandon.

In fall, I learn so much from nature and how to let go and surrender to new growth. Trees release their leaves and flowers go to seed in full faith that the fallow time to come will allow the natural process to begin again. I have, at times, held tight to relationships, jobs, and stories that no longer serve me for fear of uncertainty and change. In doing so, I withhold the opportunity for new growth from myself and the world. Conversely, when I stay curious, explore new experiences, and grapple with new ideas, I am scattering seeds in hope of a riot of color in spring.

What way of doing or being in the world no longer serves you? What would it feel like to release it to ready the conditions for new growth?

...the "road closed"
sign turned me
toward terrain I
needed to travel.

I once pushed for the creation of a new role that I thought I wanted. I presented to the school board, advocated to administration, and shared what it could look like, but at each turn it was shut down. I was hurt and angry. Looking back now, I see the path I took instead led to the more aligned and meaningful work I am doing now. Had the "road closed" sign not changed my journey, it would have certainly taken me longer to get to where I am today. I have such gratitude for the obstacles that actually became the way.

What detour on your journey has led to unexpected learnings and growth?

In a paradox, opposites
do not negate each —
they cohere in mysterious
unity at the heart of
reality.

I struggle with others who say one thing and do another or who read a room and change their personality accordingly. I think my aversion to this came from my inner work of acknowledging that I have done (and continue to do) the same, exhausting thing. I could be kind and compassionate to others, but harsh and judgmental to myself. Realizing this pushed me to embark on making my outer life match my inner world. Parker Palmer often refers to the mobius strip—a strip of paper that when one end is turned over and connected to the other, becomes a continuous loop where what seems to be the inner side, evolves to be the outer side. The inner and outer worlds interact and co-create each other. This is my urgent and ongoing work.

What experience has shone light for you on a paradox in your life? How might you allow your inner values and outer experiences to co-create with one another?

ESSENTIAL

Times of dormancy &
deep rest are essential
to all living things.

The first quiet snowfall of the season in the Midwest fills me with awe. It is like a visual hush falling over the landscape reminding me that, just like nature, I too need deep rest. Not the cat-nap-on-the-couch kind of rest, but the restorative kind of solitude that comes from allowing myself to get quiet and listen.

Bring to mind a moment when you felt rest settle into your bones. How can you gift yourself the experience of that moment again?

But for me, winter has an even greater gift.... It is the gift of utter clarity.

The beauty of winter is in its stark contrast to the abundance of the other seasons. It is my favorite time to appreciate the different personalities of trees without their robes of leaves—wise old oaks, majestic maples, and playful young willows. Their branches hold space, reaching and swaying in all types of winter weather. The crisp, cold sunlight makes the snow dazzlingly brilliant, reminding me that a season of going quiet and relinquishing things I no longer need is an act of beauty itself.

When have you been blessed with the gift of clarity? How might you create a small winter season for yourself to seek clarity?

Until we enter boldly
into the fears we most
want to avoid, those fears
will dominate our lives.

Oh, how I avoid things that scare me or that I think I am not ready for—speaking in public, stepping into a leadership role, sharing my truth. The energy I expend fearing is much better spent imagining what might happen if something goes wildly well. I have learned to do the things that scare me anyway, trusting I will learn what I need to learn from the experience. Sometimes the teaching is that it goes horribly and it wasn't meant for me! The learning is then a valuable lesson in what not to do, but for a moment, I have faced the fear and it has less power.

Name a fear that holds power or energy in your life. How might it feel to sit with it, face it directly, and learn all it has to teach you?

Spring teaches me to
look more carefully
for the green stems
of possibility.

I have a personal practice of trying to observe something as if I were going to have to draw it when it is no longer visible. It makes me pay attention to the small details, the contours, curves, and colors of a spring flower I might have lazily looked past. How often am I missing the small details embedded in ordinary days? Spring starts out muddy and messy like so many situations in life, but just below the surface are seeds waiting for a bit of warm rain and sun to sprout.

Choose an object that you use daily—a coffee cup or a favorite coat perhaps—and observe it as if you were going to draw it. What do you notice about how it changes your perspective of that thing? How might you use this practice as you go about your day?

Life is not always meant
to be measured & meted
...but to be spent from
time to time in a riot of
color and growth.

I read the children's book *Ish* by Peter H. Reynolds to my students in which the main character learns to lean into mistakes as he is drawing. This opens up his world to beautifully freeing emotions and feelings. At the end of the book, he is resting in the sun near a pond and decides not to draw—instead, he simply savors the experience. I take this wise advice with me into the world, savoring moments of connection with nature, with other humans, and with myself. It has led to appreciation and awe for the simple things that bring me joy.

When was the last time you simply savored a moment? What did it look, feel, smell, or taste like?

If you receive a gift,
you keep it alive not
by clinging to it, but
by passing it along.

I think of gifts as an exchange of energy—a piece of jewelry from your grandmother or a handmade quilt passed down through generations are priceless—but more important than family heirlooms are the stories we share with one another and the time we make to listen deeply. That is the gift that has come back to me tenfold over the years and the one I intend to continue passing along.

What is the best gift you have received and why? What act of giving has brought you the most joy and why?

Where I live, summer's
keynote is abundance.

Each summer I look forward to the early sunrises and late sunsets, a weekend day spent in, on, or near water, fresh produce from the garden, and the magical arrival of fireflies at dusk. In the midst of it, the abundance feels luxurious, but a shadow creeps in as July makes an entrance and I begin to worry about the end approaching. When in a scarcity mindset I miss all the beauty of a present moment. Nature's seasons remind me again and again that change is constant, but if I can pay attention there is so much to be learned from their reliable cycles.

What abundance do you enjoy most in the summer season?
What is helpful to you when a scarcity mindset creeps in?

The irony often tragic is that by embracing the scarcity assumption, we create the very scarcities we fear.

When I focus on scarcity, I am giving energy to lack and precluding abundance that can only emerge when I let go of proving there is not enough money, love, or joy already present in my life. I have made a practice of listing small gratitudes in a journal each morning for the previous day—a deep conversation with a friend, time to draw in the early dawn, a warm cup of coffee with cinnamon and honey. The small things are never really small, and they remind me of the true abundance of enough.

Where in your life do you experience abundance already present in small pockets of your day?

... abundance does not happen automatically. It is created when we have the sense to choose community.

A daily gratitude practice revealed the inherent abundance in my life. I have also learned that when I share time, gifts, or presence with community, the abundance expands. A beautiful truth has also been that when I share sorrow or pain, it is lessened by those who walk alongside me, not to fix me, but to deeply listen as I speak my own truth.

Can you remember a moment when a community held you up, helped you heal? How might you be in community for someone in your life right now?

Community doesn't just
create abundance—
community **IS**
abundance.

When I was struggling with health issues a few years ago, I had to lay down . . . at the end of a school year. Teachers never miss the beginning or end of a school year—it is almost sacrilege. I had no choice due to pain and I felt so guilty for not being able to be there with my students and to serve others. It was then that I was shown the abundance of community in the form of dear friends who drove me to appointments, brought me books to read, or delivered a DQ Blizzard of my choice. I realized that the community I had cultivated was there all along and exactly when I needed them. It wasn't the things they brought, but the love and belonging they enveloped me in, proving that community *is* abundance.

When have you felt wrapped in community? How did it change your experience of a difficult or joyful time in your life? How might you create community with and for others?

Summer is a reminder that... we might cease our anxious machinations & give ourselves to the abiding & abundant grace of our common life.

If you asked me what one tenet I live by or what my purpose is with the short time I have on this earth, I would tell you this: we are here to be in relationship with one another. A morning prayer I return to again and again is this: "God, may I be your eyes, ears, voice, hands, feet, and heart for someone who needs it today. May I give and receive loving kindness and grace." In our thoughts, words, and actions, our job is to be present with others, to help one another feel seen and heard, to laugh, to cry, to create community, and to walk each other home.

What simple act can you do today to help another human feel seen and heard?

GRATITUDES

THE FACT THAT THIS BOOK has made its way into the world is a dream realized for me. It stemmed from the first time I read Parker Palmer's work and only grew brighter and stronger through the years. So my first gratitude goes to Parker. Your wisdom, honesty, humor, support, and generosity have been such gifts as I have journeyed through the process of creating this work. My hope is that it honors your words, makes you smile, and introduces new readers to your work.

Thank you, Grandma Janet, for first introducing me to Parker's work, and for our countless hours reading, discussing, and laughing in your kitchen. You were the youngest ninety-six-year-old I knew, and I am sure we were soul sisters in another lifetime. I have taken up your insatiable sense of curiosity and carry it boldly wherever I go.

Jeff Crosby and Sheryl Fullerton, thank you for your generosity of time, talent, and support. Your wisdom and experience in this publishing journey have been invaluable. You are both beautiful examples of paying it forward. I am inspired by this and forever grateful.

Cindy Bunch, thanks to you and the whole team at Inter-Varsity Press for believing in this book and for your help shepherding it into the world.

To all those who have appreciated my daily drawings and asked when I was going to put them into a book—thank you for the encouragement to step out and share them more. It is incredibly meaningful to know that my very personal drawings resonate with so many on a universal level.

To my parents and in-laws, thank you for your never-ending love and support.

Sherrie, you are my sister, mirror, confidant, and indefatigable cheerleader. I can't imagine a world without you in it. To those who don't have an identical twin sister, I highly recommend it. Wonder Twin powers activate!

Spencer and Owen, thank you for always keeping me honest and making me laugh. It is an honor to see you making your way in the world as loving and compassionate young men.

Lastly, thank you, Chad, for your unwavering support, mad sense of humor, and belief in me and this project. Thank you for the countless hours of art consultation in the early weekend mornings when I kept asking which direction a limb should go, or what word should be in the circle, or who was I to be doing this. You are my favorite, and you are my love.